Golfing Jokes

Golfing Jokes

Dilwyn Phillips

Illustrations: Noel Ford
Cover design: Sion Ilar

ISBN: 9781847712301

Printed on acid-free and partly recycled paper
and published and bound in Wales by
Y Lolfa Cyf., Talybont, Ceredigion SY24 5HE
e-mail ylolfa@ylolfa.com
website www.ylolfa.com
tel (01970) 832 304
fax 832 782

Contents

Introduction

We all know that Wales is primarily a rugby nation, but golf is becoming increasingly popular nowadays. It is a well-known fact that many of our rugby heroes play golf, and the sport is set to attract more interest in the Principality with the Ryder Cup coming to the Celtic Manor Resort in 2010.

The Manor House at the resort dates back to the 1860s and first served as a family home. It was then used as a maternity hospital for 35 years. This closed in 1975 after 60,000 babies had been born there – one being Sir Terry Matthews, Wales' first billionaire and the resort's owner.

For the few that know nothing about golf, it is an outdoor game in which players hit a small hard ball with clubs that consist of a metal shaft and a wooden or metal head. The object is to strike the ball with a club so that the ball goes into a hole in the ground marked with a flag. It is played on grass and divided into 18 holes, each with a tee from where the first stroke is made. After 18 holes, the player with the lowest number of strokes is the winner of that round.

I understand that the word 'golf' has its origins in the medieval Dutch word 'kolf' or 'kolve', meaning 'club'. It is believed that word passed to the Scots, whose old dialect transformed the word into 'golve', 'gowl' or 'gouf'. By the 16th century, the word 'golf' had emerged.

It is an urban legend that the word 'golf' is derived from **G**entlemen **O**nly **L**adies **F**orbidden. Many women will say that men perpetuate this legend to enable them to continue making 'golf widows'.

I read a quote once that said, 'Golf is like a love affair: if you don't take it seriously it's not fun. If you do take it seriously it breaks your heart.'

The man that invented golf and said it was 'fun' is the same guy that invented bagpipes and said it was 'music'.

Competitive golf is played mainly on a five-and-half-inch course; i.e. the distance between the left ear and the right ear.

Golf is an easy game; it's just hard to play.

The most famous golf shot ever must surely be Alan Shepard hitting a ball on the moon in 1971, watched by an audience of millions. Does this make golf the first sport in space?

During the Battle of Britain, the St Mellon's Golf and Country Club adopted a set of unusual rules for unusual circumstances, such as:

- In competition, during gunfire or while bombs are falling, players may take shelter without penalty for ceasing play.
- A player whose stroke is affected by the simultaneous explosion of a bomb may play another ball under penalty of one stroke.

Apparently this was all done tongue in cheek, and many other clubs had the same rules.

These DIY golf books usually cancel each other out. One book tells you to keep your eye on the ball, the next says not to bother. Personally, I have a much better idea: ditch the teach-yourself books and have a titter on the tee with this one. I hope you enjoy it as much as I did collecting the stories from my golfing pals.

Dilwyn Phillips

Golf

Tickets for the British Open are hard to get and the touts have a field day. One keen spectator was offered a ticket for £100.

'That's absurd,' the enthusiast declared. 'Why, I could get a woman for that!'

'True sir,' the tout replied, 'but with this ticket you get eighteen holes!'

* * *

Dai told the greenkeeper, 'I dropped my bottle of Scotch out of the bag somewhere on the seventh. Anything handed in at lost-and-found?'

'Only the golfer who played after you, sir.'

* * *

The party games were a triumph and now the marble tournament was in full swing. Then six-year-old Tommy missed an easy shot and let fly with a potent expletive.

'Tommy,' his mother remonstrated in embarrassment from the sidelines, 'what do little boys who swear when they are playing marbles turn into?'

'Golfers,' Tommy replied.

* * *

Then there's the Cardi who gave up golf after 20 years when he lost his ball.

* * *

Fairway [faer-wai]: An unfamiliar tract of closely mown grass running directly from tee to green. Your ball can usually be found immediately to the left or right of it.

* * *

Why is it that the same golfer who can't add when it comes to the family budget at home turns into a mathematician on the golf course?

* * *

The only sure way to find a drive sliced deep into the woods is to hit a provisional ball 260 yards down the middle.

* * *

Dai is getting married and is standing by his bride to be at the church. Alongside him are his golf clubs and bag.

She whispers, 'Why have you brought your golf clubs with you?'

Dai replies, 'This is not going to take all day is it?'

* * *

The prospective bride rushed up to the prospective groom on the first tee. Ianto looked at her bridal finery and said, 'I told you: only if it rained.'

* * *

Two long-time golfers were standing overlooking the river. Alun looked to Wil and said, 'Look at those idiots fishin' in the rain.'

* * *

Q: What is the difference between a lost Titlest and the G-spot?
A: A man will spend five minutes looking for the golf ball.

* * *

Q: What do you call a blonde golfer with an IQ of 125?
A: A foursome.

* * *

The best wood in most golfers' bags is the pencil.

* * *

Ianto muttered: 'I wish I could play my normal game... just once.'

* * *

A 'gimmie' can best be defined as an agreement between two golfers… neither of whom can putt very well.

* * *

An interesting thing about golf is that no matter how badly you play, it is always possible to get worse.

* * *

'Your trouble is that you're not addressing the ball correctly.'
'Yeah, well I've been polite to the bloody thing for long enough.'

* * *

A reporter speaking to Jack Nicklaus said, 'You're spectacular, and your name is synonymous with the game of golf. You really know your way around the golf course. What's your secret?'
   Nicklaus replied, 'The holes are numbered.'

* * *

A golfer has one advantage over a fisherman: he doesn't have to produce anything to prove his story.

* * *

A golf club walks into a local bar and asks the barman for a pint of beer. The barman refuses to serve him.

'Why won't you serve me?' asks the golf club.

'You'll be driving later,' replies the bartender.

* * *

Meirion sits in clubhouse bar thinking about his next extra-marital affair. Deep in thought about the subject, he absent-mindedly starts thinking aloud.

'Not worth it,' he mutters, 'never as good as you hoped. Expensive and above all drives the wife berserk.'

A friend who was sitting close by at the time and overheard Meirion's words leaned across and said, 'Come on, Meirion, you knew what to expect when you took up golf.'

* * *

Ianto goes on holiday to Cyprus and falls in love with a beautiful girl from the Rhondda Fach. They spend the whole week together and both are so infatuated with each other that they discuss the continuation of their relationship.

'Well,' said Ianto, 'I suppose it's only fair to tell you that I'm a golf fanatic; I live, eat and sleep golf.'

'In that case,' said Mair, 'I'll be honest with you and confess to being a hooker.'

'Oh, that's no problem,' said Ianto, 'it's probably because you're not keeping your wrists together when you hold the club.'

*   *   *

'Ianto, why don't you play golf with Dai any more?' his wife asked.

'Would you play golf with a chap who moved the ball with his foot when he thought you weren't watching?' Ianto replied.

'Well, no,' admitted his wife.

'And neither will Dai,' replied the dejected husband.

*   *   *

Ianto comes home from work and is greeted by his wife dressed in a sexy little nightie.

'Tie me up,' she purrs, 'and you can do anything you want.'

So he ties her up and goes out for a round of golf.

*   *   *

Dafydd takes the day off work and decides to go out golfing. He is on the second hole when he notices a frog sitting next to the green. He thinks nothing of it and is about to shoot when he hears, 'Ribbit. Nine iron.'

Dafydd looks around and doesn't see anyone so he prepares for his shot again.

'Ribbit. Nine iron.'

He looks at the frog and decides to listen to it. He puts his other club away and grabs a nine iron. Boom! He hits a birdie. He is shocked, and says to the frog, 'Wow, that's amazing. You must be my lucky frog, eh?'

The frog replies, 'Ribbit. Lucky frog. Lucky frog.'

Dafydd decides to take the frog with him to the next hole. 'What do you think, frog?' he asks.

'Ribbit. Wood.' was the reply.

Dafydd takes out a wood and – Boom! – a hole-in-one. He is amazed and doesn't know what to say. By the end of the day, Dafydd has played the best game of golf in his life. He says to the frog, 'OK…where to next?'

The frog replies, 'Ribbit. Casino.'

They go to the casino and Dafydd says, 'OK, frog, now what?'

The frog says, 'Ribbit. Roulette.'

Upon approaching the table, Dafydd asks the frog, 'What do you think I should bet?'

The frog replies, 'Ribbit. £300 black six.'

Now this was a million-to-one shot but after the golf game, Dafydd figures, 'What the heck.'

Boom! Tons of cash come sliding back across the table.

Dafydd takes his winnings and books into the best room in the hotel. He sits the frog down and says, 'Frog, I don't know how to repay you. You won me all this money and I am forever grateful.'

The frog replies, 'Ribbit. Kiss me.'

'Why not,' Dafydd figures. 'The frog deserves it after all it's done for me.'

All of a sudden the frog turns into the most gorgeous 16-year-old girl in the world.

'And that, your honour, is how the girl ended up in my room.'

* * *

A student hitchhiker was picked up by a guy in a big Bentley Continental and noticed a bunch of golf tees on the front seat. He asked, 'What are those things for?'

The driver said, 'They're to hold my balls while I drive.'

'Boy,' exclaimed the student, 'these Bentleys have everything, don't they?'

* * *

The junior executives and staff of the company generally play football; the middle-level managers are more interested in tennis and the top management usually has a preference for golf.

MORAL OF THE STORY: As you go up the corporate ladder, the balls reduce in size.

*   *   *

Then there was the golfer who was sentenced to be hanged. He asked the warden if he could take a few practice swings first. **t.'**

*   *   *

A guy is at the driving range having a heck of a day. Everything thing he tries to hit he tops, with the ball only going about 20 feet and burning worms the whole way. Disgusted, he turns finally to the pro on the range and mutters, 'If I don't connect with this one, I'm gonna jump in that lake and drown myself!'

The pro looks at him and says, 'I don't think you can do that.'

'Why not?' the guy asks.

'I don't think you can keep your head down that long!'

*   *   *

Ianto: My wife's fed up with me playing golf and she suggested that I take up a new sport this summer.

Dai: Well, that's nice. It shows that she has your
        interests at heart. Did she make any suggestions?

Ianto: As a matter of fact, she did. By the way, how do
        you play this Russian Roulette?

* * *

The position of your hands is very important when playing golf. I use mine to cover up my scorecard.

* * *

I gave Ianto a golf lesson yesterday. He did really well. In just one lesson he was throwing my clubs as well as someone who's been playing for years!

* * *

A golfer is a confused soul who talks about women when he's playing golf, and about golf when he's with a woman.

* * *

Old golfers never die, they just lose their balls.

* * *

How do we know that the game of golf was invented in Scotland? Well, the whole point of the game is to hit the ball as few times as possible in the course of a round, and any Scotsman can tell you that the fewer times you hit a ball the longer it will last.

* * *

Wales' worst golfer hit a ball into an absolutely huge bunker.

'What club shall I use?' he asked the caddy.

'Never mind the club,' the caddy answered, 'just take along plenty of food and water.'

* * *

Golf is great. Why, just yesterday I was only two strokes away from a hole-in-one...

Gentlemen Only...

The club secretary was apologetic. 'I'm sorry, sir, but we have no tee times open on the course today.'

'Now just a minute,' the member rejoined, 'what if I told you Prince Andrew and partner wanted a game. Could you find a starting time for them?'

'Yes, of course I would.'

'Well, I happen to know that he's in Scotland at the moment, so we'll take his tee time.'

* * *

Two golfers from the Valleys were discussing a bill that Dafydd, the hospital administrator, had sent Efan, recently a father for the first time.

'I mean, £25 for use of the delivery room's just not on, old man. You know I didn't get the wife there in time and the baby was born on the front lawn.'

Dafydd leant over, took the bill, crossed out the offending entry and substituted another which read: 'Green Fee: £25.'

* * *

Ianto went out to play golf every Saturday and Sunday. It didn't matter what kind of weather it was; he was hooked on the game.

One Saturday he left the house early and headed for the golf course, but it was so bitterly cold that he decided he wouldn't play that day and went back home. Myfanwy was still in bed when he got there so he took off his clothes, snuggled up to his wife's backside and said, 'Terrible weather out there.'

She replied, 'Yeah, and can you believe my stupid husband went out to play golf?'

* * *

Some friends were playing a round of golf when they heard shouts in the distance. Looking across, they watched amazed as a buxom lady ran onto the fairway, pulled off some of her clothes and sprinted off up the course. Not two minutes later, two men in white coats appeared and asked which way the woman had gone. They pointed up the course and the two men ran off in that direction.

Bemused, the golfers carried on with their game but were again disturbed by another man. This one was staggering over the hill and panting with the effort of carrying two buckets of sand. Between wheezes, the newcomer also asked which way the woman had gone, and then tottered away. Increasingly baffled, the golf party ran after the figure.

'What the hell is going on?' they asked.

Gasping, the man explained: 'The lady has escaped from our treatment clinic. She has acute nymphomania, and as soon as she gets all her clothes off, the nearest man is ravished.'

'But why do you need two buckets of sand?' shouted the golfers after him.

'Well, I caught her the last time she escaped,' panted the man. 'This time I needed a handicap.'

* * *

Ianto and Dai had just finished the first nine and it was obvious that Ianto was having a bad day.

'Hey, Ianto, you're just not your old self today. What's the matter?' asked Dai.

Ianto, looking pretty miserable, said, 'I think Megan's dead.'

'Bloody hell, that's terrible,' said Dai. 'Hang on, you *think* your wife is dead? Aren't you sure?'

'Well,' responded Ianto, 'the sex is the same, but the dishes are piling up.'

* * *

Dai is waiting to tee off for the start of his round when he sees Will just finishing his. Dai can't help but notice that Will is wet all over the front of his trousers. Curiosity gets the better of him, so he asks Will how he got so wet. Will tells him the following story:

That day, Will had played golf for the first time with bifocals. All day long, he could see two sizes for everything. There was a big club and a little club; a big ball and a little ball, etc. Therefore, Will said that he hit the little ball with the big club and it went straight and long all day. On the green, he putted the little ball into the big cup. He said that he'd played the best golf of his life.

Dai said, 'I understand that, but how did you get all wet?'

'Well,' said Will, 'when I got to the 16th, I had to have a leak awfully bad. I went into the woods and unzipped my fly. When I looked down, there were two of them also – a big one and a little one. Well, I knew the big one wasn't mine, so I put it back.'

* * *

After a particularly poor game of golf, a popular club member skipped the clubhouse and started to go home. As he was walking to the parking lot to get his car, a policeman stopped him and asked, 'Did you tee off on the 16th hole about 20 minutes ago?'

'Yes,' the golfer responded.

'Did you happen to hook your ball so that it went over the trees and off the course?'

'Yes, I did. How did you know?' he asked.

'Well,' said the policeman very seriously, 'your ball flew out onto the highway and crashed through a driver's windshield. The car went out of control, crashing into five other cars and a fire truck. The fire truck couldn't make it to the fire so the building burned down. So, what are you going to do about it?'

The golfer thought it over carefully and responded, 'I think I'll close my stance a little bit, tighten my grip and lower my right thumb.'

* * *

Evan was playing golf at a very exclusive club in Gwynedd for the first time, and on the sixth hole he hit a hole-in-one. Jubilant, he walked down to the green. But just as he was taking his ball from the cup, up popped a leprechaun.

'Sor,' the leprechaun bowed politely and continued, 'this is a very exclusive course, and being as it faces the Emerald Isle it has everything, including the services of a leprechaun. As you made a hole-in-one on the sixth, I will be delighted to grant you any wish your heart desires.'

'Bloody hell,' said Evan in shock. But seeing the leprechaun waiting so patiently, he thought for a minute then admitted shyly that he did have a wish. 'I want to have a longer penis,' he confided.

'Your wish is granted, Sor,' the leprechaun said, and disappeared in a puff of green smoke down the hole.

Evan headed back to join up with his friends, and as he walked he could feel his penis slowly growing. The golf game progressed and Evan's penis kept getting longer and longer until it came out beneath his shorts and reached down below his knees.

'Hmm,' Evan thought, 'maybe this wasn't such a great idea after all.'

So he left his friends and went back to the sixth hole with a bucket of balls and began to shoot. Finally he hit a hole-in-one. By the time he got down to the green, he had to hold his penis to keep it from dragging on the ground. But he managed to take the ball from the cup and sure enough, out popped the leprechaun.

'Sor, this is a very exclusive course,' said the leprechaun bowing once again, 'and it has everything including the services of a leprechaun… Oh, it's you again. Well, what will it be this time?'

'Could you give me some platform shoes?' pleaded Evan.

* * *

Gareth was touring North Wales with his golf clubs and was playing on a small course near Caernarfon. He was on the first green and about to putt when he was suddenly beset by a flock of seagulls.

'Piss off will you,' he cried, thrashing at the birds.

A sweet little old lady who was knitting on a bench near the green came over to speak to him.

'Excuse me,' she said, 'there's no need to speak to the little birdies like that. All you need to say is "Shoo shoo, little birdies" then the bastards will piss off themselves.'

* * *

A married man was having an affair with his secretary. One day their passions overcame them and they took off for her house where they made passionate love all afternoon. Exhausted from the wild sex, they fell asleep and awoke around 8pm. As the man threw on his clothes, he told the woman to take his shoes outside and rub them through the grass and dirt. Mystified, she nonetheless complied and he slipped on his shoes and drove home.

'Where have you been?' demanded his wife when he entered the house.

'Darling,' replied the man, 'I can't lie to you. I've been having an affair with my secretary and we've been having sex all afternoon. I fell asleep and didn't wake up until 8 o'clock.'

The wife glanced down at his shoes and said, 'You lying bastard! You've been playing golf!'

* * *

Suddenly there was crashing and clattering, then Dafydd came into the house with his golf clubs, scowling and cussing.

'What's the matter, *cariad*, you have a bad day on the golf course?' asked Megan.

'Aye, what a rotten day! What a rotten round of golf! Why, I only hit two good balls all day, and I wouldn't have hit them if I hadn't stepped on the rake in the garage!'

. * * *

Ianto, a Valleys man, and Efan, a North Walian, were talking about playing golf during the various seasons of the year.

'In most parts of the north we cannot play in the winter time,' Efan said. 'We have to wait until spring.'

'Why, in the Rhondda we can even play in the winter time,' said Ianto. 'Snow and cold are no object to us.'

'Well, what do you do, paint your balls black?' asked Efan.

'No,' replied Ianto, 'we just put on an extra sweater or two.'

* * *

Dai and his friend Efan are halfway through a round of golf in Cardiganshire when a golf ball arrives out of nowhere and strikes Dai on the back of his head.

'Ouch!' Dai cries out, rubbing the back of his head.

Almost immediately, Ianto arrives to apologise. But Dai is having none of it.

'You call yourself a golfer?' yells Dai. 'If I had my way, I'd ban you from every golf club in Cardigan. Do you see what you've done to me? My head is bleeding. I'm going to call my solicitor as soon as I get to the clubhouse. I'll sue you for £5,000.'

'But,' says Ianto, 'didn't you hear me? I shouted "FORE".'

'OK,' says Dai, 'I'll take it.'

* * *

This guy is stranded on a desert island all alone for ten years. One day, he sees a speck on the horizon. He thinks to himself, 'It's not a ship.'

The speck gets a little closer and he thinks, 'It's not a boat.'

The speck gets even closer and he thinks, 'It's not a raft.'

Then out of the surf comes this gorgeous woman wearing a wet suit and scuba gear. She comes up to the guy and says, 'How long has it been since you've had a cigarette?'

'Ten years!' he says.

She reaches over and unzips a waterproof pocket on

her left sleeve and pulls out a pack of fresh cigarettes. He takes one, lights it, takes a long drag, and says, 'Man, oh man! Is that good!'

Then she asks, 'How long has it been since you've had a drink of whiskey?'

He replies, 'Ten years!'

She reaches over, unzips a waterproof pocket on her right sleeve, pulls out a flask and gives it to him. He takes a long swig and says, 'Wow, that's fantastic!'

Then she starts unzipping the long zipper that runs down the front of her wet suit and says to him, 'And how long has it been since you've had some REAL fun?'

The man replies, 'My God! Don't tell me that you've got golf clubs in there!'

* * *

Ianto stood over his tee shot for what seemed an eternity looking up, looking down, measuring the distance, figuring the wind direction and speed… driving his partner nuts. Finally his exasperated partner says, 'What the hell is taking so long? Hit the damned ball!'

Ianto answers, 'My wife is up there watching me from the clubhouse. I want to make this a perfect shot.'

'Give me a break! You don't stand a snowball's chance in hell of hitting her from here.'

* * *

Off the seventh tee, Dafydd sliced his shot deep into a wooded ravine. He took his eight iron and clambered down the embankment in search of his lost ball. After many long minutes of hacking at the underbrush he spotted something glistening in the leaves. As he drew nearer, he discovered that it was an eight iron in the hands of a skeleton! Dafydd immediately called out to his friend: 'Efan, I've got trouble down here!'

'What's the matter?' Efan asked from the edge of the ravine.

'Bring me my wedge,' Dafydd shouted. 'You can't get out of here with an eight iron!'

* * *

Sion was about to tee off on the golf course when he felt a tap on his shoulder. A man handed him a card that read, 'I am a deaf-mute. May I play through, please?'

Sion angrily gave the card back and communicated that no, he may NOT play through, and that his handicap did not give him such a right. Then he whacked the ball onto the green and left to finish the hole.

Just as he was about to putt the ball into the hole he was hit on the head with a golf ball, laying him out cold. When he came to a few minutes later, he looked round and saw the deaf-mute sternly looking at him, one hand on his hip, the other holding up four fingers.

*   *   *

A doctor, a lawyer and a manager were discussing the relative merits of having a wife or a mistress.

The doctor says: 'It's better to have a wife because the sense of security lowers your stress and is good for your health.'

The lawyer says: 'For sure a mistress is better. If you have a wife and want a divorce, it causes all sorts of legal problems.'

The manager says: 'You're both wrong. It's best to have both so that when the wife thinks you're with the mistress and the mistress thinks you're with your wife, you can go and play a round of golf.'

*   *   *

Ianto joins an exclusive golf club. On his very first day of playing he dials the clubhouse and shouts into the phone: 'Get me a coffee ready for when I come in!'

A voice responds, 'You fool, you've dialled the wrong extension! Do you know who you're talking to, dumbo?'

'No,' replies Ianto.

'It's the membership secretary of the golf club, you fool!'

Ianto shouts back, 'And do YOU know who YOU are talking to, you fool?'

'No,' replies the secretary indignantly.

'Good!' replies Ianto, and puts down the phone.

* * *

Myfanwy and her husband Ianto went for counselling after 30 years of marriage. When asked what the problem was, Myfanwy went into a passionate, painful tirade listing every problem she had experienced in the 30 years they had been married. She went on and on and on: neglect, lack of intimacy, emptiness, loneliness, feeling unloved and unlovable – an entire laundry list of unmet needs she had endured over the course of their marriage.

After allowing this to go on for a while the therapist got up, walked around the desk and, after asking Myfanwy to stand, unbuttoned her blouse, embraced her, put his hands on her breasts and kissed her passionately as Ianto watched with a raised eyebrow.

Myfanwy buttoned up her blouse and quietly sat down as though in a daze.

The therapist turned to Ianto and said, 'This is what Myfanwy needs at least three times a week. Can you manage that?'

Ianto thought for a moment and replied, 'Well, I can drop her off here on Mondays and Wednesdays, but on Fridays I play golf.'

* * *

Ianto got home from his Sunday round of golf later than normal and feeling very tired.

'Bad day at the course?' his wife asked.

'Everything was going fine,' he said. 'Then Dai had a heart attack and died on the tenth tee.'

'Oh, that's awful!'

'You're not kidding. For the whole back nine it was hit the ball, drag Dai, hit the ball, drag Dai… '

* * *

The room was full of pregnant women and their partners, and the class was in full swing. The instructor was teaching the women how to breathe properly, along with informing the men how to give the necessary assurances at this stage of the plan.

The teacher then announced: 'Ladies, exercise is good for you. Walking is especially beneficial. And, gentlemen, it wouldn't hurt you to take the time to go walking with your partner!'

The room became very quiet. Finally Geraint, who was in the middle of the group, raised his hand.

'Yes?' asked the teacher.

'Is it all right if she carries a golf bag while we walk?'

* * *

Ianto was at the country club for his weekly round of golf. He began his round with an eagle on the first hole and a birdie on the second. On the third hole he had just scored his first ever hole-in-one when his cell phone rang. It was a doctor notifying him that his wife had just been involved in a terrible accident and was now in a critical condition in intensive care. Ianto told the doctor to inform his wife where he was and that he'd be there as soon as possible.

As he hung up he realized he was leaving what was shaping up to be his best ever round of golf. He decided to get in a couple of more holes before heading to the hospital. He ended up finishing all 18, shooting a personal best of 61. This beat his previous best by more than ten strokes and shattered the club record by five.

Ianto was jubilant, then he remembered his wife. Feeling guilty he dashed to the hospital. He saw the doctor in the corridor and asked about his wife's condition. The doctor glared at him and shouted, 'You went ahead and finished your round of golf, didn't you! I hope you're proud of yourself! While you were out for the past four hours enjoying yourself at the country club, your wife has been languishing in the ICU! It's just as well you went ahead and finished that round because it will be more than likely your last! For the rest of her life she will require around-the-clock care. And you'll be her caregiver!'

Ianto was feeling so guilty he broke down and sobbed.

The doctor started to snicker and said, 'Just kidding! She died more than two hours ago. What'd you score?'

* * *

Ianto, who worked at a driving range, picked up a couple of dozen old balls one day and took them home with him, stuffing them into his trouser pockets. On the bus on his way home, an elderly lady sat down next to him so he had to scrunch them up to make room for her. He noticed after a while the lady was glancing sideways toward his pockets. A bit embarrassed, he said to the lady, 'It's all right ma'am, they're just golf balls.'

She nodded and smiled sympathetically, and a few moments later said, 'Oh dear, if it's anything like tennis elbow it must be painful.'

* * *

Efan the dentist was also a golf fanatic and would often take time off work to play a round. One day, he told his secretary to cancel all his appointments. She was also to leave the following voicemail message on his phone:

'Dr Benjamin is fully occupied today as he needs to fill 18 cavities. Please ring tomorrow for an appointment. Thank you.'

* * *

After hacking his way around a course with a professional golfer, Ianto asked him what the problem was with his game. The pro answered coolly and casually: 'It's simple, you're standing too close to your ball… after you've hit it!'

Hear the one about the bad-tempered Dolgellau golfer who bought a new set of Great Big Bertha woods? After playing with them for a couple of rounds he returned to his pro shop and told the pro that these were the best clubs he had ever played with. 'In fact,' he said, 'I can throw these clubs 40 yards further than my old ones.'

* * *

Geraint went to see his doctor because he was suffering from major stress syndrome. The doctor asked him if he played golf, to which he replied, 'I play at it; it's a very frustrating game, but I love it.' The doctor told him that the next time he played he should use an imaginary ball. Geraint was a little embarrassed but he decided to give it a try.

At the golf club, he explained to his buddy Gareth that his doctor had told him to play a round of golf with an imaginary ball to relieve his stress. Since it was working well, his buddy Gareth said he had stress too and asked if it would be all right if he played with an imaginary ball. Geraint said, 'Sure!'

They approached the 18th hole, a short par four, and their scores were level. Gareth teed his imaginary ball, took a stroke, and started jumping up and down shouting, 'Ace! I win!'

Geraint only turned to him, smiled, and said, 'No, I won… that was my ball.'

* * *

Myfanwy walked into the bedroom and found Ianto in bed with his golf clubs. Seeing the astonished look on her face, Ianto calmly said, 'Well, *cariad*, you said I had to choose, right?'

...Ladies Forbidden

Dai's wife went away on a golfing trip. He sent her a text message saying, 'I'm so miserable without you it's almost like you're here.'

* * *

Driving to a new golf club, Megan took several wrong turns. When she finally found the right road, she asked her husband, 'Why didn't you tell me I was lost?'

'I thought you knew where you were going,' he replied. 'You always know where you're going when I'm driving.'

* * *

Myfanwy asked Megan, 'Why are you so late for this game of golf?'

Megan replied, 'It's Sunday. I had to toss a coin between going to church or playing golf and it took 25 tosses to get it right!'

* * *

Myfanwy was out golfing one day when she hit her ball into the woods. She went into the woods to look for it and found a frog in a trap. The frog looked up at her and said, 'If you release me from this trap, I will grant you three wishes.'

Not a person to miss a trick, Myfanwy immediately freed the frog. The frog thanked her and said, 'I'm sorry but I failed to mention that there is a condition to your wishes – that whatever you wish for yourself, your husband will get ten times more or better!'

Myfanwy replied, 'That's OK – I'm happy to accept your condition. For my first wish, I want to be the most beautiful woman in the world.'

The frog warned her, 'You do realise that this wish will also make your husband the most handsome man in the world? Women will flock to him like bees to honey.'

Myfanwy replied, 'It's not a problem because I will be the most beautiful woman and he will only have eyes for me.'

So 'KAZAM!' – Myfanwy is the most beautiful woman in the world!

For her second wish, Myfanwy asked to be the richest woman in the world. The frog said, 'That will make your husband the richest man in the world and he will be ten times richer than you.'

Myfanwy said, 'It's not a problem because what's mine is his and what's his is mine.'

So 'KAZAM!' – Myfanwy is the richest woman in the world!

The frog then enquired about her third wish, to which Myfanwy answered, 'I'd like a mild heart attack.'

* * *

Two lady golfers were approaching the first tee. Myfanwy goes into her golf bag to get a ball and says to Megan, 'Hey, why don't you try this ball?' She pulls a green golf ball out of her bag. 'Use this one – you can't lose it!'

Megan replies, 'What do you mean you can't lose it?'

Myfanwy replies, 'I'm serious, you can't lose it. If you hit it into the woods it makes a beeping sound, if you hit it into the water it produces bubbles, and if you hit it on the fairway, smoke comes up in order for you to find it.'

Obviously Megan doesn't believe Myfanwy, but Myfanwy shows Megan all the possibilities until Megan is convinced.

Megan says, 'Wow! That's incredible! Where did you get that ball?'

Myfanwy replies, 'I found it.'

* * *

A group of Penrhyndeudraeth golfers were approaching the first tee when they noticed a woman being given first aid. One of the golfers asked what had happened and was informed that the woman had been stung by a bee and was having a bad reaction.

'Where was she stung?' he asked.

'Between the first and second holes,' was the reply.

'Wow! She must have been standing right over the hive.'

* * *

Bethan, Megan and Morfydd are passing by the half-open door to the men's changing rooms at the local golf club when they can't help noticing a man with his face obscured by the towel he is using to dry his hair. However, they do get quite a good view of his naked body from the waist down.

Later, Bethan says, 'Well, I didn't see his face but he's certainly not my husband!'

Megan says, 'And he isn't mine, either!'

Morfydd says, 'Hell, he isn't even a member of the club!'

* * *

A couple of women were playing golf one sunny Saturday morning at Borth and Ynyslas. The first of the twosome teed off and watched in horror as her ball headed directly toward a foursome of men playing up the 18th hole. Indeed, the ball hit Ianto and he immediately clasped his hands together at his crotch, fell to the ground and proceeded to roll around in evident agony.

The woman rushed down to Ianto and began to apologize. She explained that she was a physical therapist. 'Please allow me to help. I know I could relieve your pain if you'd allow me,' she told him earnestly.

'Ummph, oooh, nooo, I'll be alright… I'll be fine in a few minutes,' replied Ianto breathlessly as he remained in the foetal position still clasping his hands together at his crotch.

But she persisted, and Ianto finally allowed her to help him. She gently took his hands away and laid them to the side, loosened his trousers and put her hands inside. She began to massage him and after a while asked: 'How does that feel?'

To which Ianto replied: 'It feels great, but my thumb still hurts like hell.'

*   *   *

One lady golfer tells another: 'Hey, guess what! I got a set of golf clubs for my husband!'
The other replies, 'GREAT swap!'

*   *   *

A woman from Aberystwyth is learning how to play golf. She has been teaching herself to play for more than three months but she is still really bad. She decides to consult a golf pro.

When she sees the pro, she explains how bad she is and he tells her to go ahead and hit the ball. She does. The ball goes about 50 yards into the rough, slicing to the right.

The pro says to the woman, 'I can see that you have a

lot of problems. Your stance is bad, your head is all over the place, and the worst thing is that grip.'

When she asks what can be done to fix the situation, he suggests, 'Grab the club gently as if you were grabbing your husband's penis. When the feeling is right, go ahead and swing.'

She does just that and the ball goes off the tee perfectly straight for about 275 yards.

The pro says to the woman, 'That is unbelievable! I didn't think you would do that well. But now to the next problem: how do we get that golf club out of your mouth?'

* * *

The schoolteacher was taking her first golfing lesson.
'Is the word spelt "p-u-t" or "p-u-t-t"?' she asked the instructor.

'"P-u-t-t" is correct,' he replied. '"Put" means to place a thing where you want it. "Putt" means merely a vain attempt to do the same thing.'

* * *

Ifor and Megan got married, and Ifor asked Megan if he could have a dresser drawer of his own that she will never open. Megan agreed.

After 25 years of marriage, she notices that the drawer

has been left open. She takes a quick look inside and sees three golf balls and about a £1,000 cash. She confronts Ifor and asks for an explanation.

He says, 'Every time I was unfaithful to you, I put a golf ball in the drawer.'

She calculated that three times in 25 years wasn't all that bad as there had been very happy times, so she asked, 'But what about the £1,000 cash?'

Ifor answered, 'Whenever I got a dozen golf balls, I sold them for a £1.'

* * *

On wall in ladies' toilet in the golf club: 'My husband follows me everywhere.'

Written just below it: 'No I don't.'

* * *

One day a blonde was walking down the street when the club pro saw her out of the corner of his eye and yelled, 'Do you want to play?'

She said, 'No, I don't know how to. I don't even know how to hold the caddy.'

* * *

Three girls from Swansea apply for membership to a local golf club, and are told that they will be asked a simple question for which an explanation of the answer will also be required.

Blodwen goes first. She is shown a cauliflower, a potato and a knife, and is asked to explain which is the odd one out and why. She thinks for a while and answers, 'The knife, because the other two are sort of round, but the knife is long.' This answer is accepted.

Next goes Myfanwy, who also says the knife. However, her explanation was that two were vegetables whilst the knife was mineral.

Mari is asked the same question and after a few minutes of thinking, answers, 'The cauliflower – you can make chips with the other two!'

* * *

I'm not saying Myfanwy's game is bad, but if she grew tomatoes they'd come up sliced.

* * *

The golf pro walked over to two women and asked, 'Are you here to learn how to play golf?'

Myfanwy replied, 'My friend Megan is. I learned yesterday.'

* * *

Two women were put together as partners in the club tournament and met on the putting green for the first time. After introductions the first golfer asked, 'What's your handicap?'

'Oh, I'm a scratch golfer,' the other replied.

'Really!' exclaimed the first woman, suitably impressed that she was paired up with her.

'Yes, I write down all my good scores and scratch out the bad ones!'

* * *

A lady golfer goes into the pro shop and looks around, frowning. Finally the pro asks her what she wants.

'I can't find any green golf balls,' the lady golfer complains.

The pro looks all over the shop and through all the catalogues. Finally he calls the manufacturers and determines that, sure enough, there are no green golf balls.

As the lady golfer walks out the door in disgust, the pro asks her, 'Before you go, could you tell me why you want green golf balls?'

'Well, obviously because they would be so much easier to find in the bunkers!'

* * *

Four lady golfers went into the clubhouse after playing 18 holes of golf to be greeted by the lady captain. She asked them, 'Did you girls have a good game today?'

The first one said, 'Yes, I had three riders today.'

The second lady said, 'I had the most riders ever. I had five.'

The third lady said, 'I had seven riders, the same as last time.'

The last woman said, 'I beat my old record. I had 12 riders today.'

Another golfer, who happened to be at the bar and had heard the ladies talking about their game, went to the lady captain and said, 'I have been playing golf for a long time and thought I knew all the terminology of the game, but what's a rider?'

The lady captain said, 'A rider is when you hit the ball far enough to get in the golf cart and ride to it.'

* * *

Dai and Ianto are on the fourth green when Ianto misses a three-foot putt for the hole. He yells out, 'Shit!'

Two nuns are just about to tee off on the adjacent fifth hole, and one of them comes over and says, 'There's no need to use such profanity – it's only a game.'

The guy says, 'OK, I'm sorry, but I missed a putt which I thought I'd get.'

Anyway, he agrees to watch his language and everyone goes their separate ways.

As they get to the 15th hole, they notice that the nuns are just about to tee off on the 16th. The first nun tees up and hits a beauty of a drive straight on to green. The second nun tees up, slices her drive and the ball goes straight in the lake.

'Shit!' she yells.

Ianto walks over to her and tells her that she shouldn't use such profane language because it's only a game.

The nun nods her head and then says, 'I know, I know, but you only missed a simple putt; I hit my ball into the middle of the f*****g lake.'

* * *

Two old golfers in the clubhouse.

The first one says, 'You know, when I was 30 and got a hard-on I couldn't bend it at all. By the time I was 40 I could bend it about 10 degrees if I tried really hard. By the time I was 50 I could bend it about 20 degrees, no problem. I'm gonna be 60 next week, and now I can almost bend it in half with just one hand.'

'So,' says the second golfer, 'what's your point?'

'Well,' says the first, 'I'm just wondering how much stronger I'm gonna get!'

* * *

Megan goes to confession and says, 'Father, I have sinned. Last week I was playing golf and I used a profanity.'

The priest asks her to explain herself.

'Well, Father, I teed off the first and sliced the ball into the trees.'

'Ah, so that's when you swore?' says the priest.

'No,' replies Megan, 'luckily I had a clear view to the fairway. I took an eight iron, but I topped the ball and it went into a bunker!'

'So you lost your temper and used bad language?' he says.

'Goodness no,' retorts Megan, 'I was walking towards the bunker when a kestrel swooped down, picked up the ball and dropped it about 18 inches from the hole.'

The priest holds his head in his hands and says, 'Megan, you missed the f*****g putt, didn't you?'

* * *

Myfanwy is having a game of golf with a priest. At a short par three the priest asks, 'What are you going to use on this hole, Myfanwy?'

Myfanwy replies, 'An six iron, Father. How about you?'

The priest says, 'I'm going to hit a soft seven and pray.'

Myfanwy hits her six iron and puts the ball on the

green. The priest tops his seven iron and dribbles the ball a few yards.

Myfanwy comments,' I don't know about you, Father, but in my church when we pray, we keep our heads down.'

* * *

Myfanwy screamed at Alun: 'If you ever spent a Sunday with me instead of playing golf, I swear I would drop dead!'

'There's no point in trying to bribe me,' replied Alun.

Titters on the tee

One autumn day, Dave was out raking leaves when he noticed a hearse going down the street. This was followed by another hearse, followed by a man walking solemnly along, followed by a dog, and then about 200 men walking in single file. Intrigued, Dave went up to the man following the second hearse and asked who was in the first one.

'My wife,' the man replied.

'I'm sorry,' said Dave. 'What happened to her?'

'My dog bit her and she died.'

Dave was taken aback. 'And who's in the second hearse?'

'My mother-in-law. My dog bit her too and she died as well.'

Dave asked, 'Can I borrow your dog?'

'Get in line,' the man said.

* * *

The police are called to Gareth's house in Rhiwbina – the neighbours have heard some screaming. When the police arrive, they find Gareth's wife Myfanwy standing over Gareth's lifeless body, holding a six iron in her hand. The club is still dripping blood.

A police constable asks Myfanwy, 'Is that your husband, madam?'

'Yes it is,' she replies.

'And did you hit him with that golf club you're holding, madam?'

'Certainly,' replies Myfanwy. She then drops the golf club, puts her hands over her face and begins to cry. 'We only just got back from playing at a golf tournament,' she sobs.

'How many times did you hit your husband, madam?' asks the constable.

'I don't know,' replies Myfanwy. 'Six, seven, maybe even eight times – but just put me down for a six.'

*   *   *

Evan and Marian took on 18-year-old Myfanwy as a lodger. When Myfanwy asked if she could have a bath, Marian told her they didn't have a bathroom but that she could use a tin bath in front of the fire. 'Monday's the best night, when Evan goes out to the golf club,' she said, so Myfanwy agreed to have a bath the following Monday.

After Evan had gone to the golf club for a pint with the boys, Marian filled the bath and watched as Myfanwy got undressed. She was surprised to see that Myfanwy *bach* didn't have any pubic hair and told Evan when he came home. Evan didn't believe her so Marian said, 'Next week, I'll leave a gap in the curtains so that you can see for yourself.'

The following Monday, while Myfanwy again got undressed, Marian filled the bath and asked her: 'Do you shave?'

'No,' said Myfanwy, 'I've just never grown any hairs down there. Do you have hairs?'

'Oh yes,' said Marian, and she showed off her great, hairy muff.

When Evan got back inside, Marian asked him: 'Did you see?'

'Yes,' he said. 'But why the f **k did you have to show her yours?'

'Why?' she said. 'You've seen it all before.'

'I know,' he said, 'but my f ** king golfing buddies hadn't.'

* * *

There was a proper Oriental businessman visiting his newly acquired business in mid Wales. As a gesture of good will, the executives of the business took him out to a golf course for a round of golf. The man had never played the game before.

Upon his return home, his family asked what he had done in Wales. The man replied, 'Played most interesting game. Hit little white ball with long stick in large cow pasture…' He continued, 'Name of game is "Oh Shit".'

* * *

An alien spaceship hovered over a golf course. Two aliens were watching a solitary golfer practising. He was a new golfer and they watched in amazement as he duffed his tee shot, shanked his second into the rough, took three to get out of the rough onto the fairway, sliced the next shot into the bushes and took a putter to get it out on the fairway again.

Meanwhile, one alien told the other that he must be playing some sort of game and they continued to observe.

The golfer then hit a shot into a bunker by the green. He took several shots to get out of the bunker and finally onto the green. He putted several times until he finally got the ball in the hole. At this stage, ET told his partner, 'Wow, now he is in serious trouble.'

* * *

Geraint took his wife to play her first game of golf. Not surprisingly, Marged promptly hacked her first shot right through the window of a large house adjacent to the course.

Geraint cringed, 'I warned you to be careful! Now we'll have to go and apologize and see how much your lousy drive is going to cost us!'

So the couple walked up to the house and knocked

on the door. A warm voice said, 'Come on in!' When they opened the door they saw the damage that was done: glass all over the place and a broken antique bottle lying on its side near the window.

A man reclining on the couch asked, 'Are you the people that broke my window?'

'Uh… yeah. We're very sorry about that,' Geraint replied.

'Oh, no apology is necessary. Actually I want to thank you. You see, I'm a genie, and I've been trapped in that bottle for a thousand years. Now that you've released me I'm allowed to grant three wishes. I'll give you each one wish, but if you don't mind, I'll keep the last one for myself.'

'Wow, that's great!' Geraint said. He pondered for a moment then blurted out, 'I'd like a million pounds a year for the rest of my life!'

'No problem,' said the genie, 'you've got it, it's the least I can do. And I'll guarantee you a long and healthy life too! And now you, young lady, what do you want?' the genie asked.

'I'd like to own a gorgeous house complete with servants in every country in the world!' Marged said.

'Consider it done,' the genie said. 'And your homes will always be safe from fire, burglary and natural disasters!'

'And now, genie,' Geraint asked, 'what's your wish?'

'Well, since I've been trapped in that bottle and

haven't been intimate with a woman for more than a thousand years, my wish is to go to bed with your wife.'

Geraint looked at his wife and said, 'Well, *cariad*, we now have a fortune and all those houses. What do you think?'

She mulled it over for a few moments and said, 'You know, you're right. Considering our good fortune, I guess I wouldn't mind. But what about you, Geraint?'

'You know I love you, *cariad*,' replied Geraint. 'I'd do the same for you too!'

So the genie and Marged went upstairs where they spent the rest of the afternoon enjoying each other. The genie was simply insatiable.

After about three hours of non-stop fun, the genie rolled over, looked directly into Marged's eyes and asked, 'How old are you and your husband?'

'Why, we're both thirty,' she responded breathlessly.

'Really? Thirty years old and you both still believe in genies!'

* * *

Three blondes were walking through the woods when they came upon a set of tracks.

'Looks like deer tracks,' said one blonde.

'No, it looks like a cow track,' another blonde suggested.

'Actually, I think they are just dog tracks,' the third blonde offered.

They were still arguing when the train hit them!

* * *

On their silver anniversary, Megan said to Ianto: 'Do you remember when you proposed to me I was so overwhelmed that I didn't talk for an hour?'

Ianto replied: 'Yes, *cariad*, that was the happiest hour of my life.'

* * *

Evan turned around to Ianto after a round and said he was rather concerned because he'd received a letter from a man who said if he didn't stop seeing his wife, he'd break his legs.

'Well, Evan,' replied Ianto, 'are you going to stop seeing her?'

'It's not as easy as that,' replied Evan, 'he didn't sign the letter.'

* * *

Little Dafydd and his grandfather are raking leaves when Dafydd sees an earthworm trying to get back into its hole. He says, 'Grandpa, I bet I can put that worm back in that hole.'

The grandfather smiles and says, 'I'll bet you a pound you can't. It's too wiggly and limp to put back in that little hole.'

Dafydd runs into the house and comes back out with a can of hairspray. He sprays the worm until it is straight and stiff as a board. Then he stuffs the worm back into the hole.

The grandfather, impressed with his grandson's ingenuity, hands him the pound... then grabs the hairspray and runs into the house.

Thirty minutes later, the grandfather comes back out and hands Dafydd another pound.

Dafydd says, 'Grandpa, you already gave me a pound.'

The grandfather replies, 'Yes, I know. But that's from your grandma!'

* * *

A woman reported the disappearance of her husband to the police. The officer in charge looked at the photograph she handed him, questioned her, and then asked if she wished to give her husband any message if they found him.

'Yes,' she replied readily, 'tell him my mother didn't come after all.'

* * *

There was this petrol station in Llanbrynmair trying to increase its sales, so the owner put up a sign saying: 'Free sex with every full tank of petrol.'

Ianto pulled in, filled his tank, and then asked for his free sex. The owner told him to pick a number from one to ten, and if he guessed correctly he would get his free sex. Ianto guessed eight and the proprietor said, 'Sorry sir, you were close. The number was seven. Sorry, no free sex this time, but maybe next time.'

Some days later Ianto, along with his friend Ceri, pulled in again for a fill-up, and again Ianto asked for free sex. The proprietor again gave him the same story and asked him to guess the correct number. Ianto guessed two this time, and the proprietor said, 'Sorry, it was three. You were close, but no free sex this time.'

As they were driving away, Ianto said to Ceri, 'I think that game is rigged and he doesn't give away free sex at all.'

Ceri replied, 'No, it's not rigged – my wife Myfanwy won twice last week.'

* * *

One day Ianto was playing a round of golf with the vicar.

On the first hole, Ianto hits the ball into a sand bunker.

'Damn, I missed,' he says.

The vicar says, 'You shouldn't say that. It is bad.'

Later, on the ninth hole, Ianto hits the ball into the water.

'Damn, I missed,' he says again.

The vicar says, 'Don't say that. Next time you do, God will strike you down with a lightning bolt.'

On the last hole, Ianto hits it an inch short of the hole.

'Damn, I missed,' he says once again.

The vicar looks up to the sky as the clouds start to split apart. Then a lightning bolt comes down from Heaven, striking and killing the vicar.

'Damn, I missed,' God's voice echoes.

* * *

As a young man, Lefi was an exceptional golfer. At the age of 26, however, he decided to become a priest and joined a rather peculiar Order. He took the usual vows of poverty and chastity, but his Order also required that he quit golf and never play again. This was particularly difficult for Lefi, but he agreed and was finally ordained a priest.

One Sunday morning, the Reverend Father Lefi woke up, and realizing it was an exceptionally beautiful and sunny early spring day, decided he just had to play golf. So he told the associate pastor that he was feeling sick and convinced him to say Mass for him that day.

As soon as the associate pastor left the room, Father

Lefi headed out of town to a golf course about forty miles away. This way he knew he wouldn't accidentally meet anyone he knew from his parish. Setting up on the first tee he was alone. After all, it was Sunday morning and everyone else was in church!

At about this time, St Peter leaned over to the Lord while looking down from the heavens and exclaimed, 'You're not going to let him get away with this, are you?'

The Lord sighed and said, 'No, I guess not.'

Just then Father Lefi hit the ball and it shot straight towards the pin, dropping just short of it, then it rolled up and fell into the hole. It was a 420-yard hole-in-one!

St Peter was astonished. He looked at the Lord and asked, 'Why did you let him do that?'

The Lord smiled and replied, 'Think about it. Who on earth can he tell?'

* * *

The Pope met with the College of Cardinals to discuss a proposal from Shimon Peres, the former leader of Israel.

'Your Holiness,' said one of the cardinals, 'Mr Peres wants to determine whether Jews or Catholics are superior by challenging you to a golf match.'

The Pope was greatly disturbed as he had never held a golf club in his life.

'Not to worry,' said the cardinal, 'we'll call America

and talk to Jack Nicklaus. We'll make him a cardinal and he can play Shimon Peres. We can't lose!'

Everyone agreed it was a good idea. The call was made and, of course, Jack was honoured and agreed to play.

The day after the match, Nicklaus reported to the Vatican to inform the Pope of his success in the match.

'I came in second, your Holiness,' said Nicklaus.

'Second?' exclaimed the surprised Pope. 'You came in second to Shimon Peres?'

'No,' said Nicklaus, 'second to Rabbi Woods.'

* * *

Dai's wife is in bed with her lover Ianto, who also happens to be Dai's best friend. After making love, while they're just lying there, the phone rings. Since it is Dai's house, his wife picks up the phone. Ianto looks over at her and listens, only hearing her side of the conversation...

'Hello? Oh, hi, *cariad.* I'm so glad that you called,' she says, speaking in a cheery voice. After a pause, she continues: 'Really? That's great. I am so happy for you, that sounds terrific...Great...Thanks...Okay... Bye, love you.'

Dai's wife hangs up the telephone and Ianto asks, 'Who was that?'

'Oh,' she replies, 'that was Dai telling me all about the wonderful time he's having on the golf course with you.'

* * *

A famous golfer parked his brand-new Ferrari outside the Celtic Manor and went inside to book in. About ten minutes later a blonde ran up to him, shouting, 'I just saw someone steal your sports car!'

'Did you try to stop him?' asked the golfer.

'No,' said the blonde, 'I did better than that; I got the registration number of the car!'

* * *

Ianto was engrossed in a magazine while Myfanwy was reading the newspaper. Suddenly she burst out laughing.

'Get this,' she said. 'Some fella's put an ad in the paper offering to swap his wife for a season ticket to the stadium.'

'Hmm,' Ianto mumbled, still engrossed in his magazine.

Wanting to test him, Myfanwy asked, 'Would you swap me for a season ticket?'

'Absolutely not!' he said.

'That's so sweet,' she replied. 'Tell me why not.'

'Heck, the season's more than half over!' he replied.

* * *

After years of saving, Dafydd turned to Sonia and said, '*Cariad*, we've saved enough money to buy that car we started saving for in 1983.'

'You mean my brand-new Audi?' retorted Sonia.

'No,' replied Dafydd, 'a 1983 Audi!'

* * *

Myfanwy and Megan are driving down the road in a sports car. Myfanwy knows that she's speeding so she asks Megan if there's a police car behind them. Megan looks behind and sees that there is, so Myfanwy asks if he's got his lights on.

Megan replies, 'Yes... no... yes... no... yes... no... '

* * *

As Myfanwy is leaning out of the window, she sees little Tommy driving a reluctant cow down the lane.

'Where are you taking that cow?' asks Myfanwy.

'I'm taking it down to the bull,' Tommy replies.

'Couldn't your father do that?' enquires Myfanwy.

'No,' says Tommy, 'it has to be the bull!'

Older golfers

Two ninety-year-old men, Efan and Ianto, have been buddies all their lives. When it's clear that Ianto is dying, Efan visits him every day. One day Efan says, 'Ianto, we've played golf on Saturdays together for so many years. Please do me a favour. When you get to Heaven, can you try and let me know if they have any golf courses there?'

Ianto looks up at his friend from his death bed and says, 'Efan, you've been my best buddy for many years. If it's at all possible, I'll do this favour for you.'

Shortly after that, Ianto passed away.

At midnight a couple of nights later, Efan is awakened from a sound sleep by a blinding flash of white light and a voice calling out to him: 'Efan, Efan!'

'Who is it? Efan asks, sitting up suddenly.

'Efan – it's me, your buddy Ianto.'

'You're not Ianto. Ianto just died.'

'I'm telling you, it's me. Ianto,' insists the voice.

'Ianto! Where are you?'

'In Heaven,' replies Ianto. 'I have some really good news and some really bad news.'

'Tell me the good news first,' says Efan.

'The good news,' Ianto says, 'is that there are plenty of golf courses in Heaven. Better yet, all of our old buddies who died before us are members, the fairways are green and the greens plush. There are no hazards, bunkers – nothing to spoil your game. Better than all of that, we're all young again! Even better again, it's always springtime; it never rains or snows. And best of all, we can play golf all we want and we never get tired.'

'That's fantastic,' says Efan. 'It's beyond my wildest dreams! So what's the bad news?'

'You're playing in a fourball with us on Tuesday.'

*   *   *

Four old friends met one Saturday morning for a game of golf in the Rhondda.

'These hills are getting steeper as the years go by,' one complained.

'These fairways seem to be getting longer, too,' wheezed the second.

'And somehow, the bunkers seem to be bigger than I remember them,' said the third.

Having listened to his friends' complaints, the oldest of the four responded quietly and wisely: 'Oh, my friends, just be thankful we're still on this side of the grass!'

*   *   *

An elderly couple are playing in the annual club championship. They are playing a play-off hole and it is down to a six-inch putt that the wife has to make. She takes her stance and her husband can see her trembling. She putts and misses; they lose the match.

On the way home in the car her husband is fuming. 'I can't believe you missed that putt!' he says. 'That putt was no longer than my willy.'

The wife looked over at her husband, smiled and said, 'Yes dear, but it was much harder!'

* * *

Geraint, an octogenarian who was an avid golfer, moved to a new town in the South Wales Valleys and joined the local golf club. He turned up for the first time to play but was told there wasn't anybody he could play with because they were already out on the course. He repeated several times that he really wanted to play. Finally the vice captain said he would play with him and would give him a twelve-stroke handicap. Geraint said, 'I really don't need a handicap as I have been playing quite well. The only real problem I have is getting out of bunkers.'

Coming onto the 18th, Geraint hit a long drive but it landed in one of the bunkers around the hole. Taking his stroke from the bunker, he hit a very high ball which landed on the green and rolled into the hole!

The vice captain walked over to the bunker where his opponent was still standing. He said, 'Nice shot, but I thought you said you have a problem getting out of bunkers?'

Geraint replied, 'I do! Please give me a hand.'

*　*　*

When Dai retired, he was given a set of golf clubs by his co-workers. Thinking he'd give it a go, he asked the local pro for lessons, explaining that he knew nothing whatever of the game. The pro showed him the stance and swing then said, 'Just hit the ball toward the flag on the first green.'

Dai teed up and smacked the ball straight down the fairway and onto the green, where it stopped inches from the hole. 'Now what?' he asked the speechless pro.

'Uh… you're supposed to hit the ball into the cup,' the pro finally said, after he was able to speak again.

'Oh great! Now you tell me,' said Dai in a disgusted tone.

*　*　*

Ianto, who was also an avid golfer, found himself with a few hours to spare one afternoon at Royal Porthcawl. He figured if he hurried and played very fast, he could get in nine holes before he had to go home.

Just as he was about to tee off, an old gentleman shuffled onto the tee and asked if he could accompany the young man as he was golfing alone. Not being able to say no, he allowed the old gent to join him. To his surprise the old man played fairly quickly. He didn't hit the ball far but plodded along consistently and didn't waste much time.

They reached the eighth fairway and Ianto found himself with a tough shot. There was a large pine tree right in front of his ball – directly between his ball and the green. After several minutes of debating how to hit the shot, the old man finally said, 'You know, when I was your age I'd hit the ball right over that tree.'

With that challenge placed before him, Ianto swung hard and hit the ball up, right smack into the top of the tree trunk. It thudded back on the ground not a foot from where it had originally lain.

The old man offered one more comment: 'Of course, when I was your age that pine tree was only three-feet tall.'

* * *

'How was your golf game, dear?' asked Jack's wife Morfydd.

'I was hitting pretty well but my eyesight's now so bad that I couldn't see where the ball went,' he said.

'Well, you are 75 years old, Jack!' admonished his

wife. 'Why don't you take my brother Efan along?'

'But he's 85 and doesn't even play golf any more,' protested Jack.

'But he's got perfect eyesight. He could watch your ball,' Morfydd pointed out.

So the next day, Jack teed off with Efan looking on. Jack swung, and the ball disappeared down the middle of the fairway.

'Do you see it?' asked Jack.

'Yup,' Efan answered.

'Well, where is it?' yelled Jack, peering off into the distance.

'I can't remember.'

* * *

Dai and Rebecca make a vow that whoever dies first will come back and inform the other of the afterlife. Their fear is that there is no afterlife.

Many, many years later, Dai dies and, true to his word, he makes contact.

'Rebecca… Rebecca,' he says, 'can you hear me?'

'Is that you, Dai?' asks Rebecca.

'Yes, *cariad*,' he replies, 'I've come back, just as we agreed.'

'So what's it like, Dai?' asks Rebecca.

'Well, *cariad*, it's like this,' replies Dai. 'Every morning, I get up and have sex. I have breakfast and then go off to the golf course where I have sex. I sunbathe and then have sex twice. I have lunch, another romp around the golf course, then sex all afternoon. After dinner it's the golf course again, then I have sex until late. It's like this every day.'

'Oh Dai,' says Rebecca, 'you really must be in Heaven.'

'Not exactly, *cariad*,' says Dai, 'I'm a rabbit on the Celtic Manor golf course.'

* * *

Dai and Blodwen are celebrating their 50th wedding anniversary. Dai turned to Blodwen and said, 'Blod *fach*, I was wondering – have you ever cheated on me?'

Blodwen replies, 'Well, Dai, why would you be asking such a question after 50 years of happy marriage? You don't really want to know… '

'Yes, Blod, I really do. Please tell me.'

'Well, all right then. Yes, three times… '

'Three? Well, when were they?' Dai asked.

'Well, Dai, remember when you were 35 years old and you really wanted to buy a shop and no bank would give you a loan? Then remember one day Mr Ianto Evans, the bank manager himself, came over to the house and signed the loan papers, no questions asked?'

'Oh, Blod *fach*, you did that for me! I respect you even more than ever, to do such a thing for me. So, when was number two?'

'Well, Dai, remember when you had that last heart attack and you were needing that very tricky operation, and no surgeon would touch you? Then remember how Dr Williams, the heart specialist, came all the way up here to do the surgery himself, and then you were in good shape again?'

'I can't believe it! Blod *fach*, you did such a thing for me to save my life. I couldn't have a more wonderful wife. To do such a thing you must really love me, darling. I couldn't be more moved. So, all right then, when was number three?'

'Well, Dai, remember a few years ago when you really wanted to join the golf club but you were twenty-three votes short?'

* * *

Meirion was golfing one day and was struck by lightning. He died and went to Heaven. Saint Peter told him when he arrived at the gates of Heaven that the bolt of lightning was actually meant for his golf partner. But because God doesn't want it known that he makes mistakes, Meirion would have to go back to Earth as someone other than himself.

Well, Meirion thought about it for awhile and

announced to Saint Peter that he wanted to return to Earth as a lesbian. Saint Peter asked him why a macho guy like him would choose to return as a lesbian. Meirion answered, 'It's simple really, this way I can still make love to a woman, AND I can hit from the red tees!'

* * *

Meirion and Blodwen were sitting on the edge of their double bed looking out of the window at the terraced houses opposite. They had both recently retired and were enjoying the time by themselves after over 40 years of marriage.

Blodwen sighed, 'We've done OK, haven't we, Meirion *cariad*?'

'Suppose we have, yes,' he replied.

'One thing I am very proud of, Meirion.'

'What's that?'

'In the early days, every time we made love I made you pay me a pound.'

'Yes you did, Blodwen.'

'And I increased that every year in line with inflation, didn't I?'

'With inflation. Yes you did, Blodwen *bach*, you did indeed.'

'Well Meirion, I saved all that money, invested it over the years and now we own every house in this street.'

Meirion was astounded; he didn't know what to say.

Then Blodwen turned to him with a saddened look on her face. 'There is only one regret, Meirion.'

'One regret, Blodwen *cariad*; what's that?'

'If you hadn't played golf every Sunday, we'd own the pub on the corner as well.'

*　*　*

My doctor told me to play 36 holes a day, so I went out and bought an harmonica.

*　*　*

The old golfer paced anxiously up and down outside the emergency room of Bronglais Hospital, near the Aberystwyth golf course. Inside, the doctors were operating to remove a golf ball accidentally driven down a player's throat. The sister-in-charge noticed the old golfer and went to reassure him.

'It won't be long now,' she said. 'Are you a relative?'

'No, no, *cariad*,' he replied, 'it's my ball.'

*　*　*

A couple of old pensioners from Aberystwyth were golfing when one said he was going to Dr Lloyd for a new set of dentures in the morning. His friend Geraint remarked that he had gone to the same dentist a few years before.

'Is that so?' Bleddyn said. 'Did he do a good job?'

'Well, I was on the course yesterday when the fellow on the 12th hole hooked a shot,' he said. 'The ball most have been going 200mph when it hit me in the balls. That,' he added, 'was the first time in two years my teeth didn't hurt.'

* * *

Ceri goes to see his doctor. After a lengthy examination the doctor sighs, looks Ceri in the eye and says, 'I've some bad news for you, Ceri. You have an incurable heart condition. I suggest you quickly put your affairs in order.'

Ceri is initially shocked. But then, being a calm, solid character, he composes himself and quietly leaves the doctor's office. His son Geraint is waiting for him.

'Geraint,' says Ceri, 'we Welsh celebrate when things are good and we sometimes celebrate when things are not so good. In my case, Geraint, things aren't so good – I have an incurable heart condition. So I suggest we go to the golf club for a few drinks.'

Four or five glasses of whiskey later, the two are feeling a little less sad. Then, after a few laughs and some more glasses of whiskey, they are approached by two of Ceri's club mates, curious as to what Ceri and Geraint are celebrating. Ceri tells them, 'Boys, we're drinking to my impending death. I've been diagnosed with AIDS.'

His club mates are shocked. They give Ceri their condolences, have a few beers and leave.

Geraint then says, 'Hey, Dad, you tell me you're dying of a heart condition yet you tell your mates you're dying of AIDS. I don't understand. Why?'

Ceri replies, 'I don't want any of them sleeping with your mam after I'm gone.'

* * *

Twm and Efan, lifelong golfing buddies, are involved in a match-play contest with the score all-square at the 18th tee. Twm slices his tee shot way left and the ball finally stops on the cart path. Meanwhile, Efan smashes his first shot straight down the middle.

'Oh well,' says Twm, 'I should get a free drop from there.'

'Heck no,' says Efan, 'we play the ball as it lies.'

So after dropping his opponent off in the middle of the fairway, Twm takes the golf cart to his lie on the concrete path. Sparks fly from the cart path as Twm makes a few aggressive practice swings. Finally, Twm hits the ball off the cart path, leaving a miraculous shot only three feet from the pin.

As the two meet on the fairway, Efan comments, 'That was a great shot… what club did you use?'

'Your six iron,' says Twm.

* * *

'I play golf in the low 80s,' the little old man was telling one of the young boys at the club.

'Wow,' said the young man, 'that's pretty impressive.'

'Not really,' said the little old man. 'Any hotter and I'd probably have a stroke.'

* * *

THE FOUR STAGES OF LIFE

1) You believe in Santa Claus.

2) You don't believe in Santa Claus.

3) You are Santa Claus.

4) You look like Santa Claus.

Fourballs

A blonde is standing by the first tee waiting for her golf lesson from the resident professional. A foursome is in process of teeing off. Efan addresses the ball and swings, hitting it 230 yards straight down the middle of the fairway.

'That was a good shot,' said the blonde.

'Not bad considering my impediment,' said Efan.

'What do you mean?' said the blonde.

'I have a glass eye,' said Efan.

'I don't believe you. Show me,' said the blonde.

So Efan popped his eye out and showed her.

Next, Dai addresses the ball and swings, hitting it 240 yards straight down the middle of the fairway.

'That was a good shot,' said the blonde.

'Not bad considering my impediment,' said Dai.

'What's wrong with you?' asked the blonde.

'I have a prosthetic arm,' said the golfer.

'I don't believe you. Show me,' said the blonde, so he screwed his arm off and showed her.

Then Wil addresses the ball and swings, hitting it 250 yards straight down the middle of the fairway.

'That was a good shot,' said the blonde.

'Not bad considering my impediment,' said Wil.

'What's wrong with you?' the blonde asked.

'I have a prosthetic leg,' said Wil.

'I don't believe you. Show me,' said the blonde, so he screwed his leg off and showed her.

The fourth golfer, Ianto, addresses the ball and swings, hitting it 280 yards straight down the middle of the fairway.

'That was a wonderful shot,' said the blonde.

'Not bad considering my impediment,' said Ianto.

'What's wrong with you?' said the blonde.

'I have an artificial heart,' said Ianto.

'I don't believe you. Show me,' said the blonde.

'I can't show you out here in the open,' said Ianto. 'Come around here behind the pro shop.'

As they had not returned within five minutes, his golfing mates decided to go and see what was holding them up. As they turned the corner behind the pro shop, sure enough, there he was, screwing his heart out.

* * *

It was a sunny Saturday morning and Ianto was beginning his pre-shot routine. He was visualizing his upcoming shot when a voice came over the clubhouse loudspeaker: 'Would the gentleman on the ladies' tee please back up to the men's tee!'

Ianto was still deep in his routine, seemingly impervious to the interruption.

Again the announcement: 'Would the man on the

women's tee kindly back up the men's tee!'

Ianto had had enough. He shouted, 'Would the announcer in the clubhouse kindly shut up and let me play my second shot!'

* * *

Meirion joined a threesome; and as he had a very successful day he was invited back the next day for a game at 8am.

'Look boys, I'd really like to play,' said Meirion, 'but I could be two minutes late.'

Next morning he showed up right on time and played another lovely round, but this time he played every stroke left-handed. Again he was invited to join the threesome at 8am the following day.

'Aye, I'll be here,' said Meirion, 'but remember I could be a couple of minutes late. If so, it won't be more than a couple of minutes!'

'We'll wait,' one of the golfers assured him. 'But by the way, could you explain something that's been mystifying us all? Yesterday you played right-handed and today you played left-handed. Obviously you're proficient at both, so how do you decide which way to play?'

'Ah well,' Meirion answered, 'when I wake up in the morning, if my darling wife's lying on her right side, I play right-handed and if she's lying on her left side, I play left-handed. Simple as that.'

'But what if she's lying on her back?'

'Oh, that's when I'm two minutes late!'

* * *

On the fourth hole, the following conversation took place:

Dai: 'You have no idea what I had to do to be able to come out golfing this weekend. I had to promise my wife that I will paint every room in the house next weekend.'

Efan: 'That's nothing, I had to promise my wife that I will build her a new deck for the pool.'

Wil: 'Man, you both have it easy! I had to promise my wife that I will remodel the kitchen for her.'

They continued to play the hole when they realized that Ianto has not said a word. So they asked him: 'You haven't said anything about what you had to do to be able to come golfing this weekend. What's the deal?'

Ianto: 'I just set my alarm for 5:30am. When it goes off, I shut off my alarm, give the wife a budge and say, "Golf course or intercourse?" So she says, "It's cold this morning, remember to wear your sweater."'

* * *

Four gentleman who didn't know each other were paired up at the first tee and introduced themselves before teeing off. By the fourth fairway, both golf and conversation were going well with them all. Just then, a funeral procession proceeded past them on the nearby highway. One of the gentlemen stopped playing, lowered his head, and placed his hat over his heart. Once the procession had passed, the other three golfers remarked on how respectful his gesture was. The gentleman said, 'Well, I ought to be respectful. I was married to her for 45 years.'

* * *

A foursome are in the changing room of a golf club when a mobile phone on a bench starts to ring. Dafydd picks it up, engages the hands-free speaker function and says, 'Hello?'

'*Cariad*, it's me,' says a woman, 'are you at the club?'

'Yes,' replies Dafydd.

'Well, I'm at the shopping centre,' she says, 'and I've found a beautiful leather coat. It's £450. Can I buy it?'

'OK,' says Dafydd, 'go ahead and buy it if you like it that much.'

'Thanks,' she replies. 'I also stopped by the BMW dealership and had a close look at the 2010 models. I saw one that I really liked.'

'How much was it?' asks Dafydd.

'£43,000,' she replies.

'For that price,' says Dafydd, 'I'd want it with all the options.'

'Great,' she says, 'just one more thing. That house we wanted last year is back on the market. They've dropped the price to £750,000 now.'

Dafydd says, 'Well then, go ahead and buy it, but don't offer more than £720,000.'

'OK,' she says, 'I'll see you later *cariad*. I love you.'

'Bye *cariad*, I love you too,' says Dafydd and then hangs up.

The other boys in the locker room who heard

all of this conversation are looking at Dafydd in astonishment. Then Dafydd shouts out, 'Does anyone know whose mobile phone this is?'

* * *

A foursome of golfers watch a lone player play up short of the green they are on. As they tee off at the next hole they see him quickly chip on and putt out. He almost runs to the tee where the foursome is. He looks at the bewildered players and says: 'Hey boys, do you mind if I play through? I've just heard the wife has had a terrible accident.'

* * *

Four men went golfing one day. Three of them headed to the first tee while Ianto went into the clubhouse to take care of the bill. The three men started talking and bragging about their sons. Twm told the others, 'My son is a builder, and he is so successful that he gave a friend a new house for free. Just gave it to him!'

Efan said, 'My son was a car salesman, and now he owns a multi-line dealership with Rolls-Royce. He's so successful that he gave one of his friends a new Bentley, fully loaded.'

Dai, not wanting to be outdone, bragged, 'My son is a stockbroker, and he's doing so well that he gave his friend an entire portfolio.'

Ianto joined them on the tee after taking care of business. Twm mentioned, 'We were just talking about our sons. How is yours doing?'

Ianto replied, 'Well, my son is gay, and is a stripper in a gay bar.' The other three men grew silent as he continued: 'I'm not totally thrilled about the strip job, but he must be doing well. His last three boyfriends gave him a new house, a brand-new Bentley, and an entire stock portfolio.'

Mixed fours

One morning a foursome of men were waiting at the men's tee while another foursome of ladies were hitting from the ladies' tee. The ladies were really taking their sweet time. Finally, when the last woman was ready to hit the ball, she hacked it about ten feet then went over to the ball and hacked it another ten feet or so. She looked up at the men and said apologetically, 'I guess all those f*****g lessons I took this winter didn't help.'

One of the men immediately replied, 'Now that's your problem, you see. You should have taken golf lessons instead.'

* * *

Three old buddies are about to play their regular match when the starter asks if they mind that a lady joins them to make up a fourball. When they see the stunningly beautiful 18-year-old blonde they all agree that she would make a great fourth. Her standard of golf does not match her looks, however, and after playing 17 bad holes she gets to the 18th and has a 20-foot putt for a par.

'I would do anything in the world to get a par,' she tells the three men.

All three obviously have the same thing in mind. Efan says, 'Hold your hands tight together and aim about six inches to the right of the hole.'

Dai says, 'No, no, aim just inside the left edge and hit it firm, make sure you do not leave it short.'

Ianto walks around the green surveying the hole from every angle and says, 'Ah, it's a gimmie.'

* * *

Efan and Ianto are out on the course and come upon a couple of ladies playing slowly. Efan walks up towards the ladies to ask if they can play through. About halfway there, he turns around and comes back and says to Ianto, 'I can't go up there and talk to them – that is my wife and my mistress.'

So Ianto replies, 'I'll go up and ask them.'

When he is about halfway there, he turns around and comes back and states to Efan: 'Small world.'

* * *

Husband and wife were playing in the mixed foursomes. He hit a great drive down the middle – she sliced the second shot into a copse of trees. Unfazed, he played a brilliant recovery shot which went onto the green, a metre from the pin. She poked at the putt and sent it five metres beyond the pin. He lined up the long putt and sank it. To his wife he said, 'We'll have to do better. That was a bogey five.'

'Don't blame me,' she snapped, 'I only took two of them.'

*   *   *

A lovely afternoon finds one fellow and his wife golfing. They have had a wonderful time and the man has had a near-perfect game. The final hole, by far the most difficult, wraps around an old barn. With a terrible slice, the man puts the barn between his ball and the green. Knowing that the strokes it will take to get around the barn will destroy his score, he begins to rant and rave.

His wife, hating to see him ruin such a great afternoon, makes a suggestion: 'What if I were to hold open the barn doors? That way you could send it right through the barn onto the green.'

He thinks this over and decides that it will work. With his wife holding open the barn door, he lines up with the hole and gives the ball a terrific 'whack'! The ball shoots through the air and right into the head of his wife, killing her instantly.

Months go by, the man mourning all the while. His friends, hating to see him in such a state, convince him to go golfing with them. They end up at the same course and on the final hole where, oddly enough, another terrible slice puts the old barn between his ball and the green. Again he begins to rant and rave at what this dilemma will do to his score.

His friend, wanting to please him, makes a suggestion: 'What if I were to hold open the barn doors? That way you could send it right through the barn onto the green.'

'No,' the man replies, 'last time I did that I got two over par.'

* * *

While playing on the front nine of a complicated golf course, Ianto became confused as to which hole he was playing. Looking around, he saw Myfanwy playing ahead of him. He walked up to her, explained his confusion and asked her if she knew which hole he was on. She replied, 'I'm on the seventh hole, and you are a hole behind me, so you must be on the sixth hole.' Ianto thanked her and went back to his golf.

On the back nine the same thing happened, and Ianto approached Myfanwy again with the same request. She said, 'I'm on the 14th hole, and you are a hole behind me, so you must be on the 13th hole.' Once again he thanked her and returned to his play.

Ianto finished his round and went to the clubhouse where he saw the same lady sitting at the end of the bar. He asked the steward if he knew her. The steward replied that she was a sales lady and played the course often. Ianto then approached her and said, 'Let me buy you a drink in appreciation for your help. I understand that you are in the sales profession. I'm in sales, also. What do you sell?'

Myfanwy replied, 'If I tell you, you'll laugh.'

'No, I won't,' said Ianto.

'Well, if you must know,' she answered, 'I work for Tampax.'

With that, Ianto laughed so hard he almost lost his breath.

She said, 'See, I knew you would laugh.'

'That's not what I'm laughing at,' Ianto replied. 'I'm a salesman for Preparation H, so I'm still a hole behind you!'

Golf caddies

Four caddies were caddying for a golfer around Llanrhystud golf course. His friends asked him why he had so many caddies.

'It was my wife's idea,' he replied, 'she thinks I should be spending more time with the kids.'

* * *

'I want you to know that this is not the game I usually play,' snapped an irate golfer to his caddy.

'I should hope not, sir. But tell me,' enquired the caddy, 'what game do you usually play?'

* * *

'Caddy, do you think it is a sin to play golf on Sunday?'

'The way you play, sir, it's a crime any day of the week!'

* * *

One day, a Cardi went playing golf. After standing for a while on the tee, he asked the boy standing beside him: 'You are my caddy for today?'

'Yes,' answered the boy.

'Are you good at finding lost balls?'

'Oh yes, I find every lost ball!'

'Okay, boy, then run and search for one, then we can start!'

* * *

After a man came home from a long round of golf, his wife kissed him then kissed their son who came in a few moments later.

'Where's he been?' the husband asked.

'He's been caddying for you all afternoon,' the wife replied.

'No wonder he looks so familiar!'

* * *

Golfer: 'Notice any improvement today, Alun?'
Caddy: 'Yes, ma'am. You've had your hair done.'

* * *

'That can't be my ball, caddy. It looks far too old,' said the player, looking at a ball deep in the trees.

'It's a long time since we started, sir.'

* * *

After a series of disastrous holes the strictly amateur golfer, in an effort to smother his rage, laughed hollowly and said to his caddy: 'This golf is a funny game.'

'It's not supposed to be,' said the boy gravely.

* * *

On the 16th of the Llandrindod Wells course, a very careful player was studying the green. First he got down on his hands and knees to check out the turf between his ball and the hole. Then he flicked several pieces of grass out of the way and, getting up, he held up a wet finger to try out the direction of the wind. Then, turning to his caddy, he asked: 'Was the green mowed this morning?'

'Yes, sir.'

'Right to left or left to right?'

'Right to left, sir.'

The golfer putted... and missed the hole completely. He whirled on the caddy, 'What TIME?'

* * *

'That's good for one long drive and a putt,' said the cocky golfer as he teed his ball and looked down the fairway to the green. He swung mightily and hit his ball which landed about a metre from the tee.

His caddy handed him his putter and remarked: 'And now for one hell of a putt.'

*   *   *

Friendly golfer to player searching for lost ball: 'What sort of a ball was it?'

Caddy (butting in): 'A brand-new one – never been properly hit yet!'

*   *   *

Ianto believed himself a superior caddy. He certainly had a superior attitude towards the man whose clubs he carried. Why, only last month he had caddied for the club captain, and now each time his client asked for a five wood, Ianto would sneer, 'The club captain used a four iron from here.' And so it continued all the way around – the caddy recommended the clubs the captain would have used and the golfer's game went rapidly from bad to worse.

Finally, at the 18th, there was a huge lake to cross.

'OK, know-all,' said the golfer, 'what would the club captain suggest here?'

Ianto replied, 'I think if he had come this far with you, he'd say, "Use an old ball."'

*   *   *

Efan turned to his caddy and said, 'This is the worst golf course I've ever played on!'

'This isn't the golf course, sir,' replied the caddy, 'we left that an hour ago!'

Caddy, this is the worst golf course I've ever played on!

Golf course, Sir? – we left that an hour ago!

* * *

'I'd move heaven and earth to be able to break 100 on this course,' sighed Dai, the golfer.

'Try heaven,' advised the caddy. 'You've already moved most of the earth.'

* * *

'Well, Caddy, how do you like my game?'
'Very good, sir! But personally I prefer golf.'

* * *

'Well, I have never played this badly before!'
'I didn't realize you *had* played before, sir.'

* * *

'Caddy, do you think my game is improving?'
'Oh yes, sir! You miss the ball much closer than you used to.'

* * *

A pretty terrible golfer was playing a round of golf for which he had hired a caddy. The round proved to be somewhat tortuous for the caddy to watch and he was getting a bit exasperated by the poor play of his employer.

At one point the ball lay about 180 yards from the green and the as the golfer sized up his situation, he asked his caddy, 'Do you think I can get there with a five iron?'

The caddy replied, 'Eventually.'

'Please stop checking your watch all the time, Caddy.
It's distracting!'
'This isn't a watch, sir, it's a compass!'

Efan sliced his drive and watched resignedly as the ball plummeted into the woods. He followed after it and found his ball surrounded by thick undergrowth and wedged firmly between two tree roots. He contemplated the situation for a few profoundly silent minutes then turned to his caddy and asked: 'You know what shot I'm going to take here?'

'Yes, sir,' replied the boy as he took a hip flask of malt whisky from the bag.

* * *

Ianto called one of the caddies and said, 'I want a caddy who can count and keep the score. What's 3 and 4 and 5 add up to?'

'11 sir,' said the caddy.

'Good, you'll do perfectly.'

* * *

Dafydd: Would you mind wading into the pond and retrieving my ball?
Caddy: Why?
Dafydd: It's my lucky ball.

The 19th hole

A waiter at the golf club restaurant brings the golfer the steak he ordered with his thumb over the meat.

'Are you crazy,' yelled the customer, 'sticking your thumb in my steak?'

'What,' answers the waiter, 'you want it to fall on the floor again?'

*   *   *

Dafydd is on a date. He parks his car outside the clubhouse and gets his girlfriend in the back seat. They make love, but the girl wants to do it again almost instantly. They end up doing it a second, a third and a fourth time, until Dafydd needs a rest and asks his girlfriend to excuse him as he needs to take a leak.

While out of the car, he notices a man a few yards away changing a flat tyre. He walks over and says, 'Listen, my girlfriend's over there in my car and I've already given it to her four times and she still wants more. If you give her one for me, I'll change your tyre.'

The lucky motorist readily agrees, climbs into the vehicle and begins shagging the insatiable girl. While he is banging away in the doggy position, a policeman shines a torch through the window.

'What do you think you're doing there?' he asks the man, who replies, 'I'm making love to my wife.'

The policeman looks bemused and says, 'Why don't you do it at home?'

The man answers, 'Well, I didn't know it was my wife until you shone the torch on her.'

* * *

Ianto goes into the clubhouse and sits down and orders a drink. Other than the steward there's no one in the place. All of a sudden he hears a voice that says, 'Nice suit.' He looks around but doesn't see anyone, and the steward looks busy washing some glasses.

A little while later the same voice says, 'Nice tie.' Ianto looks around again and doesn't see anyone. He finally asks the steward if he just said something.

'No,' replies the steward, 'it wasn't me. It was probably the peanuts though. They're complimentary.'

* * *

Efan staggered into casualty with concussion, multiple bruises, two black eyes, and a five iron wrapped tightly around his throat. Naturally the doctor asked him, 'What happened to you?'

'Well,' Efan replied, 'I was having a quiet round of golf with my wife, when at a difficult hole we both sliced our golf balls into a field of cattle. We went to look for them and while I was looking around I noticed one of the cows had something white at its rear end. I walked over, lifted its tail, and sure enough, there was a golf ball with my wife's monogram on it – stuck right in the middle of the cow's fanny. Still holding the cow's tail up, I yelled to my wife, "Hey, this looks like yours!" I don't remember much after that.'

*　*　*

In the first year of marriage, the man speaks and the woman listens. In the second year the woman speaks and the man listens. In the third year they both speak and the neighbours listen.

*　*　*

MYFANWY: What would you do if I died? Would you get married again?
IANTO: Definitely not!
MYFANWY: Why not – don't you like being married?
IANTO: Of course I do.
MYFANWY: Then why wouldn't you remarry?
IANTO: Okay, I'd get married again.
MYFANWY (with a hurtful look on her face): You would?
IANTO: (makes audible groan)

MYFANWY: Would you live in our house?

IANTO: Sure, it's a great house.

MYFANWY: Would you sleep with her in our bed?

IANTO: Where else would we sleep?

MYFANWY: Would you let her drive my car?

IANTO: Probably, it is almost new.

MYFANWY: Would you replace my pictures with hers?

IANTO: That would seem like the proper thing to do.

MYFANWY: Would she use my golf clubs?

IANTO: No, she's left-handed.

MYFANWY: (silence)

IANTO: F**k…

* * *

Three male labradors, one brown, one golden, and one black were sitting in a waiting room at the vet's when they struck up a conversation. The black turned to the brown one and said, 'So why are you here?'

The brown lab replied, 'I'm a pisser. I piss on everything… the sofa, the curtains, the cat, the kids. But the final straw was last night when I pissed in the middle of my owner's bed.'

The black lab said, 'So what is the vet going to do?'

'Gonna cut my nuts off,' came the reply. 'They reckon it'll calm me down.'

The black lab then turned to the golden one and asked, 'Why are you here?'

The golden lab said, 'I'm a digger. I dig under fences, dig up flowers and trees, I dig just for the hell of it. When I'm inside, I dig up the carpets. But I went over the line last night when I dug a great big hole in my owner's couch.'

'So what are they going to do to you?' the black lab enquired.

'Looks like I'm losing my nuts too,' the dejected golden labrador said.

The golden lab then turned to the black one and asked, 'Why are you here?'

'I'm a humper,' the black lab said. 'I'll hump anything. I'll hump the cat, a pillow, the table, fence posts, whatever. I want to hump everything I see. Yesterday, my owner had just got out of the shower after a round of golf, and as she was bending down to dry her toes I just couldn't help myself. I hopped on and started humping away.'

The golden and brown labs exchanged a sad glance and said, 'So, nuts off for you too, huh?'

The black lab said, 'No, I'm here to get my nails clipped!'

* * *

Ianto is having a pint in the clubhouse. He gets a call on his mobile. He hangs up, grinning from ear to ear, and orders a drink for everybody in the bar.

'My wife has just produced a typical Welsh baby boy weighing 25 pounds,' he says.

Nobody can believe that any new baby can weigh in at 25 pounds but Ianto just shrugs.

'That's about average in Wales,' he says. 'Like I said, my boy's a typical Welsh baby boy.'

Congratulations were showered on him from all around and many exclamations of 'WOW!' were heard. One woman actually fainted due to sympathy pains.

Two weeks later Ianto returns to the bar.

The barman says, 'Aren't you the father of that typical Welsh baby that weighed 25 pounds at birth? Everybody's been making bets about how big he'd be in two weeks. We were going to call you… so how much does he weigh now?'

Ianto proudly answers, 'Seventeen pounds.'

The barman is puzzled and concerned. 'What happened? He weighed 25 pounds the day he was born.'

Ianto takes a slow swig from his Brains Bitter, wipes his lips on his shirt sleeve, leans into the barman and proudly says, 'Had him circumcised.'

* * *

Myfanwy was standing in the kitchen preparing to boil eggs for breakfast, wearing only the T-shirt that she normally slept in. As Ianto walked in, almost awake and ready for a round of golf, she turned and said softly, '*Cariad*, you've got to make love to me this very moment.'

Ianto's eyes lit up and he thought, 'Bloody hell, I am either still dreaming or this is going to be my lucky day.'

Not wanting to lose the moment, Ianto embraced Myfanwy and then gave it his all, right there on the kitchen table.

Afterwards Myfanwy said, 'Thanks,' and returned to the stove, her T-shirt still around her neck.

A little puzzled, Ianto asked, 'What was that all about?'

Myfanwy explained, 'The egg timer's broken.'

* * *

Ianto and Myfanwy were in chapel one Sunday. About halfway through the sermon, Myfanwy leans over and says to Ianto, 'I just let out a silent fart; what do you think I should do?'

Ianto replies, 'Put a new battery in your hearing aid.'

* * *

A middle-aged couple had two beautiful daughters but always talked about having a son. They decided to try one last time for the son they always wanted.

The wife got pregnant and delivered a healthy baby boy. The joyful father rushed to the nursery to see his new son, but he was horrified by the ugliest child he had ever seen. He told his wife: 'There's no way I can be the father of this baby. Look at the two beautiful daughters I fathered! Have you been fooling around behind my back?'

The wife smiled sweetly and replied: 'Not this time!'

*   *   *

Two women had gone for a girl's night out. Both were very faithful and loving wives, but they had become over-enthusiastic on the Bacardi Breezers.

Incredibly drunk and walking home, they needed to pee so they stopped in the cemetery. One of them had nothing to wipe with so she thought she would take off her panties and use them. Her friend, however, was wearing a rather expensive pair of panties and did not want to ruin them. She was lucky enough to squat down next to a grave that had a wreath with a ribbon on it, so she proceeded to wipe with that. After the girls had done their business they proceeded to go home.

The next day one of the women's husbands was concerned that his normally sweet and innocent wife was still in bed hungover, so he phoned the other husband and said, 'These girls nights have got to stop! I'm starting to suspect the worst. My wife came home with no panties!'

'That's nothing,' said the other husband, 'mine came

back with a card stuck to her ass that said, "From all of us at the golf club. We'll never forget you.'"

* * *

After an exhaustive review of the research literature, here's the final word on nutrition and health:
1. Japanese eat very little fat and suffer fewer heart attacks than us.
2. Mexicans eat a lot of fat and suffer fewer heart attacks than us.
3. Chinese drink very little red wine and suffer fewer heart attacks than us.
4. Italians drink excessive amounts of red wine and suffer fewer heart attacks than us.
5. Germans drink beer and eat lots of sausages and fats and suffer fewer heart attacks than us.
6. The French eat *foie gras*, full-fat cheese and drink red wine and suffer fewer heart attacks than us.
CONCLUSION: Eat and drink what you like. Speaking English is apparently what kills you.

* * *

Secrets to a happy marriage:
1. It is important to find a woman who is a good cook and also keeps a tidy house.
2. It is important to find a woman who has plenty of money and also earns a lot.

3. It is important to find a woman that likes to have sex in every known way.

MOST important:

4. These three women must NEVER meet.

* * *

Two guys were discussing the new secretary at their office during a round of golf. Ianto said to Efan: 'I went to her place last Tuesday and we had wonderful sex. She's a lot better in bed than my wife!'

Two days later on the course, Efan said to Ianto: 'Well, I went to her place too and we had sex as well, but I still think your wife is better in bed!'

* * *

A rather confident Geraint walks into the golf club bar after a good round and takes a seat next to a very attractive woman. He gives her a quick glance and then casually looks at his watch for a moment.

The woman notices this and asks, 'Is your date running late?'

'No,' Geraint replies, 'I just bought this state-of-the-art watch and I was just testing it.'

The intrigued woman says, 'A state-of-the-art watch? What's so special about it?'

'It uses alpha waves to telepathically talk to me,' he explains.

'What's it telling you now?' she asked.

'Well, it says you're not wearing any knickers,' he said.

The woman giggles and replies, 'Well, it must be broken then because I am wearing knickers!'

Geraint explains, 'Damn thing must be an hour fast.'

* * *

An American decided to write a book about famous churches around the world. For his first chapter he decided to write about British churches. So he bought a plane ticket and took a trip to London, thinking that he would work his way across the country.

On his first day he was inside a London church taking photographs when he noticed a golden telephone mounted on the wall with a sign that read '£10,000 per call'. The writer, being intrigued, asked a priest who was strolling by what the telephone was used for. The priest replied that it was a direct line to Heaven and that for £10,000 you could talk to God. The writer thanked the priest and went along his way.

Next stop was Nottingham. There, at a very large cathedral, he saw the same golden telephone with the same sign under it. He wondered if this was the same kind of telephone he had seen in London and he asked a nearby nun what its purpose was. She told him that it was a direct line to Heaven and that for £10,000 he could talk to God.

'OK, thank you,' said the writer.

He then travelled to Liverpool, Belfast, Chester, Essex, Scotland and Birmingham. In every church he saw the same golden telephone with the same '£10,000 per call' sign under it.

Upon leaving Birmingham, the American saw a sign for Cardiff and decided to see if Welsh folk had the same phone. He arrived in Cardiff and again, there was the same golden telephone, but this time the sign under it read '10p per call'. The writer was surprised so he asked the priest about the sign.

'Father, I've travelled all over Great Britain and I've seen this same golden telephone in many churches. I'm told that it is a direct line to Heaven, but in every church the price was £10,000 per call. Why is it so cheap here?'

The priest smiled and answered, 'You're in Wales now, son – it's a local call.'

* * *

Ianto arrived at the Pearly Gates carrying a heavy burden so he decided to confess his sins.

He said, 'Do you know, just before the war, I played in a golf match for Wales against England. We were drawn with the last hole to play, and my ball was less than three feet from the pin. I carefully eyed up the putt and, I'm ashamed to say, putted out whilst the pin was still in the cup. No one noticed so I carefully removed the pin and claimed the hole. Wales won the match by that one foul shot which I never declared. The team at the clubhouse all believed that I'd saved the day. I jumped up into the air triumphantly. I've kept that secret to this day; I've been very dishonest.'

'Well, come into Heaven and make yourself comfortable, Ianto.'

'But, St Peter, I don't deserve this,' said Ianto.

'Sshh, I'm not St Peter; he's on leave. I'm St David.'

* * *

A completely inebriated Ianto walked into the clubhouse. After staring for some time at the only woman seated at the bar, he walked over to her, placed his hand up her skirt and began fondling her. She jumped up and slapped him silly. He immediately apologized and explained, 'I'm sorry. I thought you were my wife. You look exactly like her.'

'Why you drunken, worthless, insufferable asshole!' she screamed.

'That's funny,' Ianto said, 'you even sound exactly like her too!'

* * *

At the clubhouse, Dai was drowning his sorrows and sent Myfanwy a text message:

'When we were together you always said you'd die for me. Now that we've broken up, I think it's time you kept your promise.'

* * *

Three golf club manufacturers had all done business for years on the same block in the small town of Newport, Gwent. After years of peaceful co-existence, the Jones shop decided to put a sign in the window saying: 'We make the best golf clubs in Wales.'

Not to be outdone, the Davies shop soon followed suit and put a sign in their window proclaiming: 'We make the best golf clubs in the world.'

Finally, the Jenkins family put a sign out at their shop saying: 'We make the best golf clubs on the block.'

* * *

Dafydd: That fellow over in the corner of the clubhouse – I wonder where he's from?

Granddad Twm: I'll go and ask him. Hello stranger, where are you from?

Stranger: I'm not from here.

Granddad Twm: First time here then, eh?

Stranger: Never have I been here before.

Granddad Twm: Where do you go to church?

Stranger: Not to the one across the street from the house, that's for sure.

Granddad Twm: Do you like Welsh choirs?

Stranger: I don't like opera.

Granddad Twm: Do you drink Welsh beer?

Stranger: I'm not drinking whisky.

Granddad Twm: Are you a member of the visiting rugby team?

Stranger: Yes, I'm not.

Dafydd: Did you find out where he is from?

Granddad Twm: He's OK, he's a Welshman.

*   *   *

Dai had the reputation of being a fantastic salesman. One day he visited a large department store in Cardiff and informed the manager: 'These golf clubs will cut your handicap by 50%.' To which the manager replied, 'That's great, I'll take two sets.'

*   *   *

Moses, Jesus and an old man are golfing. Moses steps up to the tee and hits the ball. It goes sailing over the fairway and lands in the water trap. Moses parts the water and chips the ball onto the green.

Jesus steps up to the tee and hits the ball. It goes sailing over the fairway and lands in the water trap. Jesus just walks on the water and chips the ball onto the green.

The old man steps up to the tee and hits the ball. It

goes sailing over the fairway and heads for the water trap. But just before it falls into the water, a fish jumps up and grabs the ball in its mouth. As the fish is falling back down into the water, an eagle swoops down and grabs the fish in its claws. The eagle flies over the green when a lightning bolt shoots from the sky and barely misses it. Startled, the eagle drops the fish. When the fish hits the ground, the ball pops out of its mouth and rolls into the hole for a hole-in-one.

Jesus then turns to the old man and says, 'Dad, if you don't stop fooling around we won't bring you next time.'

* * *

Three buddies stood on the first tee, ready for a game. Dai takes a swing and sends a daisy cutter 50 yards up the fairway. The club pro happened to be standing quite near to him, so Dai asked him, 'What did I do wrong?'

The pro replied, 'Loft.'

Efan tees up, swings, and hooks his ball into the rough just 25 yards away. He asks the pro, 'What did I do wrong?'

The pro replied again: 'Loft.'

Ianto takes his shot and it goes straight into the pond. Likewise he asks, 'What did I do wrong?'

Again the answer is 'Loft'.

Ianto turns to the pro and says, 'The three of us did

completely different shots and yet you gave us the same reason. What is "Loft"?'

'Lack Of F*****g Talent,' replies the pro.

* * *

A talkative golfer complained to Ianto one day about a rude fellow who was in the clubhouse with him.

'The man must have yawned four or five times while I was talking,' he said.

'Maybe he wasn't yawning,' Ianto commented. 'Maybe he was trying to say something.'

* * *

A REMINDER TO GOLFERS

1. Back straight, knees bent, feet shoulder-width apart.
2. Form a loose grip.
3. Keep your head down.
4. Avoid a quick backswing.
5. Stay out of the water.
6. Try not to hit anyone.
7. If you are taking too long, please let others go ahead of you.
8. Don't stand directly in front of others.
9. Quiet please, while others are preparing to go.
10. Don't take extra strokes.
    That's very good. Now, flush the urinal, go outside and tee off.

Golf facts and fiction

The average golf ball has 336 dimples. These assist the aerodynamics of the ball in flight.

* * *

Twelve golfers represent their continent in the Ryder Cup.

* * *

The original course at St Andrews had 22 holes.

* * *

Joyce Wethered's drive hit a swallow in 1972, then she birdied the hole. In fact you can say she had two birdies at the same hole.

* * *

Mark Twain described golf as a good walk spoiled.

* * *

The USA won the first Ryder Cup.

*   *   *

Nick Faldo scored a hole-in-one in the 1993 Ryder Cup.

*   *   *

The circumference of a golf ball is four and a quarter inches.

*   *   *

The maximum number of clubs a player can carry is fourteen.

*   *   *

The highest course in Europe is at Sestriere, Italy (6,500 feet).

*   *   *

Golf was dropped from the Olympics Games in 1908.

*   *   *

The prototype of the modern golf ball was invented by Dr Haskell in 1902.

* * *

The rules of golf were first written down in 1744.

* * *

The golf tee was invented by George Grant in 1899.

* * *

The longest hole in the world is the seventh at Satsuki Golf Course, Sano, Japan (881 metres).

* * *

Tiger Woods was six when he scored his first hole-in-one.

* * *

A North Wales golfing family hit an amazing three holes-in-one in three straight days on Llanfairfechan Golf Course, with perfect 116-yard pitches into the ninth in August 2007. The odds of achieving such a feat were 'between 10 and 15 million to one'.

* * *

The longest golf course in the world is the International Golf Club in Massachusetts.

* * *

The Tactu Golf Club in Morococha, Peru, is believed to be the highest in the world. At its lowest point, it's 14,335 feet above sea level.

* * *

Golfers nervous of huge bunkers would do well to avoid the Pine Valley Course in New Jersey. It's home to the 'Hell's Half Acre' bunker, which is believed to be the largest in the world.

* * *

Eight of the world's oldest golf clubs are owned by the Royal Troon Golf Club in Scotland.

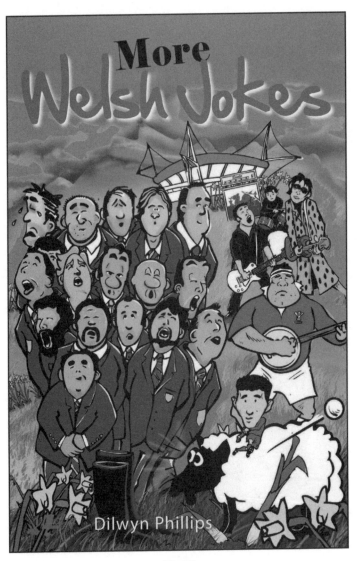

More
Welsh Jokes

Dilwyn Phillips

£3.95

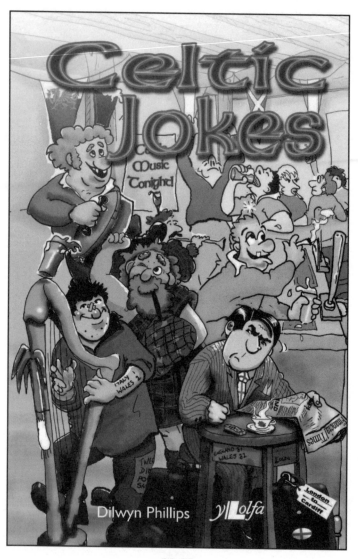

£3.95

£3.95

This book is just one of a whole range of
Welsh interest publications from Y Lolfa.
For a full list of books currently in print,
send now for your free copy of our new,
full-colour Catalogue – or simply surf into
our website

www.ylolfa.com

for secure, on-line ordering.

Talybont, Ceredigion, Cymru SY24 5HE
e-bost ylolfa@ylolfa.com
gwefan www.ylolfa.com
ffôn (01970) 832 304
ffacs 832 782